From Amanda's Kitchen to You

Amanda's Recipe Book (filled with recipes from her heart)

Copyright 2015 © Alice Tidwell

Cover by: © Mariia Pazhyna - Fotolia.com

Back Cover: © Julia and

© jokatoons – USFotolia.com

Printed in the United States

ISBN-13: 978-1515129721

ISBN-10: 1515129721

This book belongs to: _____

If found please call:_____

Email:_____

© **Matthew Cole**

Page # - Name of Recipe
1
2
3
4
5
6
7
8
9
10
11
12
13
14
15
16
17
18
19
20
21
22
23
24
25

Page # - Name of Recipe
26
27
28
29
30
31
32
33
34
35
36
37
38
39
40
41
42
43
44
45
46
47
48
49
50

Page # - Name of Recipe
51
52
53
54
55
56
57
58
59
60
61
62
63
64
65
66
67
68
69
70
71
72
73
74
75

© jokatoons

DISH NAME:_____

Oven Temp:_____ **Bake Time:_____**

INGREDIENTS AND MEASUREMENTS

DIRECTIONS:

NOTES:

DISH NAME:_____

Oven Temp:_____   **Bake Time:_____**

INGREDIENTS AND MEASUREMENTS

DIRECTIONS:

NOTES:

DISH NAME:_____

Oven Temp:_____ Bake Time:_____

INGREDIENTS AND MEASUREMENTS

DIRECTIONS:

NOTES:

DISH NAME:_____

Oven Temp:_____   Bake Time:_____

INGREDIENTS AND MEASUREMENTS

DIRECTIONS:

NOTES:

DISH NAME:_____

Oven Temp:_____   **Bake Time:_____**

INGREDIENTS AND MEASUREMENTS

DIRECTIONS:

NOTES:

DISH NAME:_____

Oven Temp:_____ Bake Time:_____

INGREDIENTS AND MEASUREMENTS

DIRECTIONS:

NOTES:

DISH NAME:_____

Oven Temp:_____ Bake Time:_____

INGREDIENTS AND MEASUREMENTS

DIRECTIONS:

NOTES:

DISH NAME:_____

Oven Temp:_____ **Bake Time:_____**

INGREDIENTS AND MEASUREMENTS

DIRECTIONS:

NOTES:

DISH NAME:_____

Oven Temp:_____   **Bake Time:_____**

INGREDIENTS AND MEASUREMENTS

DIRECTIONS:

NOTES:

DISH NAME:_____

Oven Temp:_____   Bake Time:_____

INGREDIENTS AND MEASUREMENTS

DIRECTIONS:

NOTES:

DISH NAME:_____

Oven Temp:_____ Bake Time:_____

INGREDIENTS AND MEASUREMENTS

DIRECTIONS:

NOTES:

DISH NAME:_____

Oven Temp:_____   **Bake Time:_____**

INGREDIENTS AND MEASUREMENTS

DIRECTIONS:

NOTES:

DISH NAME:_____

Oven Temp:_____   Bake Time:_____

INGREDIENTS AND MEASUREMENTS

DIRECTIONS:

NOTES:

DISH NAME:_____

Oven Temp:_____ **Bake Time:_____**

INGREDIENTS AND MEASUREMENTS

DIRECTIONS:

NOTES:

DISH NAME:_____

Oven Temp:_____   Bake Time:_____

INGREDIENTS AND MEASUREMENTS

DIRECTIONS:

NOTES:

DISH NAME:_____

Oven Temp:_____ **Bake Time:_____**

INGREDIENTS AND MEASUREMENTS

DIRECTIONS:

NOTES:

DISH NAME:_____

Oven Temp:_____ **Bake Time:**_____

INGREDIENTS AND MEASUREMENTS

DIRECTIONS:

NOTES:

DISH NAME:_____

Oven Temp:_____ Bake Time:_____

INGREDIENTS AND MEASUREMENTS

DIRECTIONS:

NOTES:

DISH NAME:_____

Oven Temp:_____   **Bake Time:_____**

INGREDIENTS AND MEASUREMENTS

DIRECTIONS:

NOTES:

DISH NAME:_____

Oven Temp:_____   **Bake Time:**_____

INGREDIENTS AND MEASUREMENTS

DIRECTIONS:

NOTES:

DISH NAME:_____

Oven Temp:_____   **Bake Time:_____**

INGREDIENTS AND MEASUREMENTS

DIRECTIONS:

NOTES:

DISH NAME:_____

Oven Temp:_____   Bake Time:_____

INGREDIENTS AND MEASUREMENTS

DIRECTIONS:

NOTES:

DISH NAME:_____

Oven Temp:_____ **Bake Time:_____**

INGREDIENTS AND MEASUREMENTS

DIRECTIONS:

NOTES:

DISH NAME:_____

Oven Temp:_____ **Bake Time:_____**

INGREDIENTS AND MEASUREMENTS

DIRECTIONS:

NOTES:

DISH NAME:_____

Oven Temp:_____   **Bake Time:_____**

INGREDIENTS AND MEASUREMENTS

DIRECTIONS:

NOTES:

DISH NAME:_____

Oven Temp:_____   **Bake Time:_____**

INGREDIENTS AND MEASUREMENTS

DIRECTIONS:

NOTES:

DISH NAME:_____

Oven Temp:_____   Bake Time:_____

INGREDIENTS AND MEASUREMENTS

DIRECTIONS:

NOTES:

DISH NAME:_____

Oven Temp:_____   **Bake Time:_____**

INGREDIENTS AND MEASUREMENTS

DIRECTIONS:

NOTES:

DISH NAME:_____

Oven Temp:_____   Bake Time:_____

INGREDIENTS AND MEASUREMENTS

DIRECTIONS:

NOTES:

DISH NAME:_____

Oven Temp:_____   **Bake Time:_____**

INGREDIENTS AND MEASUREMENTS

DIRECTIONS:

NOTES:

DISH NAME:_____

Oven Temp:_____   Bake Time:_____

INGREDIENTS AND MEASUREMENTS

DIRECTIONS:

NOTES:

DISH NAME:_____

Oven Temp:_____   **Bake Time:_____**

INGREDIENTS AND MEASUREMENTS

DIRECTIONS:

NOTES:

DISH NAME:_____

Oven Temp:_____ Bake Time:_____

INGREDIENTS AND MEASUREMENTS

DIRECTIONS:

NOTES:

DISH NAME:_____

Oven Temp:_____ **Bake Time:**_____

INGREDIENTS AND MEASUREMENTS

DIRECTIONS:

NOTES:

DISH NAME:_____

Oven Temp:_____   **Bake Time:_____**

INGREDIENTS AND MEASUREMENTS

DIRECTIONS:

NOTES:

DISH NAME:_____

Oven Temp:_____   **Bake Time:_____**

INGREDIENTS AND MEASUREMENTS

DIRECTIONS:

NOTES:

DISH NAME:_____

Oven Temp:_____   **Bake Time:_____**

INGREDIENTS AND MEASUREMENTS

DIRECTIONS:

NOTES:

DISH NAME:_____

Oven Temp:_____   **Bake Time:_____**

INGREDIENTS AND MEASUREMENTS

DIRECTIONS:

NOTES:

DISH NAME:_____

Oven Temp:_____ Bake Time:_____

INGREDIENTS AND MEASUREMENTS

DIRECTIONS:

NOTES:

DISH NAME:_____

Oven Temp:_____ Bake Time:_____

INGREDIENTS AND MEASUREMENTS

DIRECTIONS:

NOTES:

DISH NAME:_____

Oven Temp:_____   Bake Time:_____

INGREDIENTS AND MEASUREMENTS

DIRECTIONS:

NOTES:

DISH NAME:_____

Oven Temp:_____   **Bake Time:_____**

INGREDIENTS AND MEASUREMENTS

DIRECTIONS:

NOTES:

DISH NAME:_____

Oven Temp:_____   **Bake Time:_____**

INGREDIENTS AND MEASUREMENTS

DIRECTIONS:

NOTES:

DISH NAME:_____

Oven Temp:_____   **Bake Time:_____**

INGREDIENTS AND MEASUREMENTS

DIRECTIONS:

NOTES:

DISH NAME:_____

Oven Temp:_____ Bake Time:_____

INGREDIENTS AND MEASUREMENTS

DIRECTIONS:

NOTES:

DISH NAME:_____

Oven Temp:_____ **Bake Time:_____**

INGREDIENTS AND MEASUREMENTS

DIRECTIONS:

NOTES:

DISH NAME:_____

Oven Temp:_____   **Bake Time:_____**

INGREDIENTS AND MEASUREMENTS

DIRECTIONS:

NOTES:

DISH NAME:_____

Oven Temp:_____   **Bake Time:_____**

INGREDIENTS AND MEASUREMENTS

DIRECTIONS:

NOTES:

DISH NAME:_____

Oven Temp:_____   **Bake Time:_____**

INGREDIENTS AND MEASUREMENTS

DIRECTIONS:

NOTES:

DISH NAME:_____

Oven Temp:_____ **Bake Time:_____**

INGREDIENTS AND MEASUREMENTS

DIRECTIONS:

NOTES:

DISH NAME:_____

Oven Temp:_____ **Bake Time:_____**

INGREDIENTS AND MEASUREMENTS

DIRECTIONS:

NOTES:

DISH NAME:_____

Oven Temp:_____   **Bake Time:_____**

INGREDIENTS AND MEASUREMENTS

DIRECTIONS:

NOTES:

DISH NAME:_____

Oven Temp:_____ Bake Time:_____

INGREDIENTS AND MEASUREMENTS

DIRECTIONS:

NOTES:

DISH NAME:_____

Oven Temp:_____   **Bake Time:_____**

INGREDIENTS AND MEASUREMENTS

DIRECTIONS:

NOTES:

DISH NAME:_____

Oven Temp:_____   Bake Time:_____

INGREDIENTS AND MEASUREMENTS

DIRECTIONS:

NOTES:

DISH NAME:_____

Oven Temp:_____ **Bake Time:_____**

INGREDIENTS AND MEASUREMENTS

DIRECTIONS:

NOTES:

DISH NAME:_____

Oven Temp:_____ **Bake Time:_____**

INGREDIENTS AND MEASUREMENTS

DIRECTIONS:

NOTES:

DISH NAME:_____

Oven Temp:_____ **Bake Time:_____**

INGREDIENTS AND MEASUREMENTS

DIRECTIONS:

NOTES:

DISH NAME:_____

Oven Temp:_____   **Bake Time:_____**

INGREDIENTS AND MEASUREMENTS

DIRECTIONS:

NOTES:

DISH NAME:_____

Oven Temp:_____ **Bake Time:_____**

INGREDIENTS AND MEASUREMENTS

DIRECTIONS:

NOTES:

DISH NAME:_____

Oven Temp:_____ **Bake Time:_____**

INGREDIENTS AND MEASUREMENTS

DIRECTIONS:

NOTES:

DISH NAME:_____

Oven Temp:_____ **Bake Time:_____**

INGREDIENTS AND MEASUREMENTS

DIRECTIONS:

NOTES:

DISH NAME:_____

Oven Temp:_____ **Bake Time:_____**

INGREDIENTS AND MEASUREMENTS

DIRECTIONS:

NOTES:

DISH NAME:_____

Oven Temp:_____ **Bake Time:**_____

INGREDIENTS AND MEASUREMENTS

DIRECTIONS:

NOTES:

DISH NAME:_____

Oven Temp:_____   **Bake Time:_____**

INGREDIENTS AND MEASUREMENTS

DIRECTIONS:

NOTES:

DISH NAME:_____

Oven Temp:_____ **Bake Time:_____**

INGREDIENTS AND MEASUREMENTS

DIRECTIONS:

NOTES:

DISH NAME:_____

Oven Temp:_____   **Bake Time:_____**

INGREDIENTS AND MEASUREMENTS

DIRECTIONS:

NOTES:

DISH NAME:_____

Oven Temp:_____   **Bake Time:_____**

INGREDIENTS AND MEASUREMENTS

DIRECTIONS:

NOTES:

DISH NAME:_____

Oven Temp:_____   Bake Time:_____

INGREDIENTS AND MEASUREMENTS

DIRECTIONS:

NOTES:

DISH NAME:_____

Oven Temp:_____ **Bake Time:_____**

INGREDIENTS AND MEASUREMENTS

DIRECTIONS:

NOTES:

DISH NAME:_____

Oven Temp:_____   **Bake Time:_____**

INGREDIENTS AND MEASUREMENTS

DIRECTIONS:

NOTES:

DISH NAME:_____

Oven Temp:_____ **Bake Time:_____**

INGREDIENTS AND MEASUREMENTS

DIRECTIONS:

NOTES:

DISH NAME:_____

Oven Temp:_____ **Bake Time:_____**

INGREDIENTS AND MEASUREMENTS

DIRECTIONS:

NOTES:

DISH NAME:_____

Oven Temp:_____   **Bake Time:_____**

INGREDIENTS AND MEASUREMENTS

DIRECTIONS:

NOTES:

DISH NAME:_____

Oven Temp:_____ Bake Time:_____

INGREDIENTS AND MEASUREMENTS

DIRECTIONS:

NOTES:

© vitd

©All Write All Bright Books
71 Tandy Lane – Sparta, TN 38583
(931)946-1221

Made in the USA
Columbia, SC
06 February 2025

53422922R00046